ITALIC
CALLIGRAPHY
AND HANDWRITING
EXERCISES AND TEXT

LLOYD J. REYNOLDS

TAPLINGER PUBLISHING COMPANY
NEW YORK

In Memory of RICHARD KING

1901 · 1967

FOREWORD

This book is designed for the use of students and teachers who believe that they need more detailed direction in learning Italic than is available in Mr. Fairbank's *Manual* or in Mr. Benson's *The First Writing Book*. It is recommended that these three books be studied together, especially the writings of Alfred Fairbank, to whom we are all indebted for the Italic revival.

By working with the large sizes of Platignum nibs one can learn to write out bulletin board notices of rather impressive size. Also, work in the large pen sizes makes it easier for one to learn details of letter construction. Small writing tends to look better than it is, for details are not clearly seen — especially by the beginner. The recommended inks for use with the Platignum pen are the Pelikan 4001 fountain pen ink series available in brilliant black, royal blue, blue-black and green. The brilliant black is especially recommended for its jetness and even flow. For larger posters on butcher paper, Coit and Speedball pens are recommended. For notices and bulletins use Pelikan Eternal or India inks. The butcher paper requires Carbon inks. Poster colors can be diluted so that they will flow in Coit and Speedball pens. When using Speedball with poster colors, pry up the reservoir on top just so that it does not quite touch the nib.

Remember that it takes time, patience, critical practice and knowledge to learn any art or craft. No "art experience" is going to result from any busy work for a few hours experimenting with the edged pen. A project lasting six weeks is better than nothing, but only a few students will learn enough in that time to continue on their own. A few secondary schools are offering year courses in calligraphy and prepare interested students for the national competition in Italic handwriting, which is conducted by the Western American Branch of the Society for Italic Handwriting. (See the notice at the back of this book.) In time, it is hoped that both secondary schools and colleges will offer four years in calligraphy.

If the reader is interested in seeing films on calligraphy and Italic handwriting on his local educational television channel, he should write to The Division of Continuing Education, Box 1491, Portland, Oregon 97207, for information. These films can be used in schools having closed circuit television systems.

In addition to my indebtedness to Alfred Fairbank I owe much to Arnold Bank of The Carnegie Institute of Technology for his encouragement and invaluable assistance.

PLATE I

Sit facing the table, not sideways, and sit up straight.

Let the lower part of the pen rest on your middle finger and touch the pen lightly with the tips of thumb and forefinger. The upper part of the pen rests in the valley between the base knuckles of thumb and forefinger. Rest your hand on its side, not on the tip of the little finger. Let there be as little pressure as possible (1) of your fingers on the penholder, (2) of the pen nib on the paper, and (3) of the hand on the table. Watch your forefinger, let it be arched at all times. If it collapses you are pressing too hard and you will never acquire the light touch necessary to good handwriting. Get the idea, take it easy, and maintain enough wide-open concentration to be aware of your losing the idea or growing tense. Avoid rote practice. When you become tired or careless, drop it and do something else.

The axis of the wrist should be up at a steep angle and both elbows should be away from the body and should rest comfortably on the table. For right-handed persons, keep the paper straight before you (not canted) except when you are practicing Plates 13, 14, and 15. Then, as in all current cursive rapid personal handwriting, the foot of the sheet of paper is turned to the right.

Left-handed students have a choice of three methods: (1) write with the hand above the top of the paper, (2) use a "left oblique" nib and cant the foot of the sheet to the left, or, (3) use a "straight" nib as the right-handed writers do, and turn the foot of the sheet 90° clockwise. Write "from top to bottom."

Note meanings of "pen-angle" and "scale." Overlap the guide lines just a little. Five pen-widths above the writing line is the "waist line." Half-way between waist line and ascender line is the "cap" line.

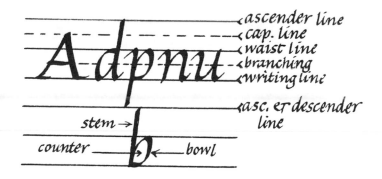

Don't let the letter slope be more than 5°. See the bottom of Plate 1.

Until you really grasp the meaning and necessity of pen-angle and scale, continue to study the first three plates.

Practice the exercises with the pen nibs indicated at the bottom of each plate from Plate 2 on, and use the corresponding guide lines. (Detach guide sheets from the back of the book and tuck them inside the folded 8½" x 11" sheets.)

Do not hurry at the beginning. Understand what you are doing, or you are only wasting time. Study the model thoroughly before you write a letter. Do not repeat the letter more than twice without putting down the pen and finding out precisely what you did wrong and what you should do to correct your mistakes.

In learning the letter forms, trace carefully and slowly the letters on Plates 2, 3, and 4. Be certain that the pen's edge matches the white lines. When you have the *feel* of the edge at a 45° angle to the writing line, squint, and with eyes almost closed, continue tracing, but concentrate on the sensations of touch and movement. Use little pressure on the heavy downstrokes and even less on the thin hair lines. Move slowly on heavy turns and downstrokes and rapidly on thin hair lines. Make your hand remember the proper touch and movement. When you can write the letter with your eyes closed, you have it. Learn to rely upon your hand's memory of the letter form rather than upon eye and hand coordination.

Try to avoid moving your fingers. Write by moving your whole hand on a free wrist. This eliminates the small muscle or finger movement, which is a problem with young children. Finger writing can produce hand cramp; hand writing avoids it. See Plate 15 for the Arcade exercise.

1. Pen-angle, scale, etc.

45°

Keep the edge of the pen at a 45° angle

10
7½
5
2½
-5

Abg136

Single stroke: abcghijklmnoqrsuv

wyœz Double stroke: defptx&yy

Letter-slope close to 5° only.

1

Examine the plates carefully, noting that each letter is written twice, once with a stylus to indicate stroke sequence and direction of pull and again with the B-4 nib. The white line indicates the *constant* angle of the *edge* of the pen. Go over the exercise repeatedly with a *dry pen*. Memorize the number of strokes for each letter, and the order and direction of strokes. The hairpin turn in the stylus-written skeleton letter (first seen on *n*, line 1, Plate 1) indicates only that the pen is not lifted. When you write, do not make this turn.

Be certain when you do this dry pen exercise that the edge of the pen always matches the angle of the white line. Note that at this pen-angle, the edge of the pen designs the thick and thin contrasts and gradations. Unless you acquire the 45° pen-angle *at the beginning,* all subsequent work will be wrong. Italic current-cursive—rapid personal handwriting—requires frequent hairline diagonal joins, and they *demand* a steep pen-angle.

Memorize the width-height relationships, and try to get not only the total *idea* of the Italic alphabet, but also the *feel* in your hand of the pen's edge on the paper as it moves, making correctly formed letters.

Note that in *n, b, p, h, k, m,* and *r* the hairline branches *out* halfway up and that in *a, d, g, q,* and *u* it branches *in* halfway up.

Use little pressure on the down strokes, only enough to keep the ink flowing. Always practice a feather-touch; float the pen. Use even less pressure on the upstroke. Go slow on the downstroke, fast on the hairline upstroke. If you hold the pen lightly enough, you will be able to get a tactile sensation of the variations in friction. Master these differences in pressure, friction, speed, and visual contrasts and gradations; and you will be started on the acquisition of a genuinely rhythmical script.

After going over the entire alphabet repeatedly with a dry pen practice the narrow, slightly sloping elliptical *o* with a pencil. Note that the part of the *o* farthest to the *left* is *low*. Remember this *o* is the key to *a, d, g, q, c,* and *e,* and see that you get similar curves on the left sides of these six letters.

Note that the part of *o* farthest to the *right* is *high*. Thus, *b* and *p* should have curves similar to the right side of *o*. See line 3, Plate 3.

Alternate *o* with *i*, first a half page in pencil, then a half page in pen and ink, using a B-4.

2. Sequence and direction of strokes

Note __D__, meaning double-stroke letters.

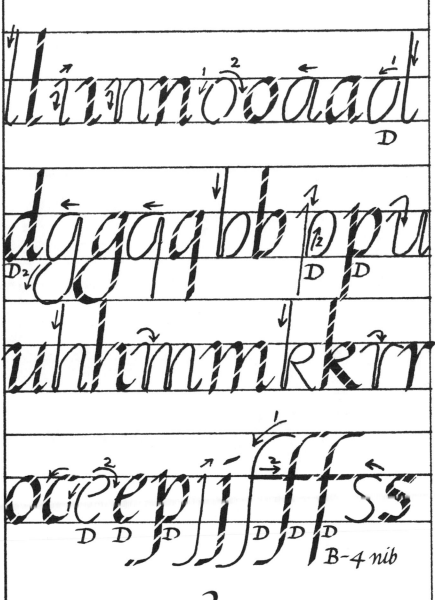

B-4 nib

Keep a turn over and down into *i* and over and up out of *i*. Avoid either a wide curve or an angle. The entrances and exits are narrowly elliptical, as is the *o*. An ellipse is a circle in perspective; its width is slightly more than half its height, and its axis slopes 5° from the vertical.

The jot over the *i* is pulled from the lower left to upper right.

3. Continuation of Plate 2.

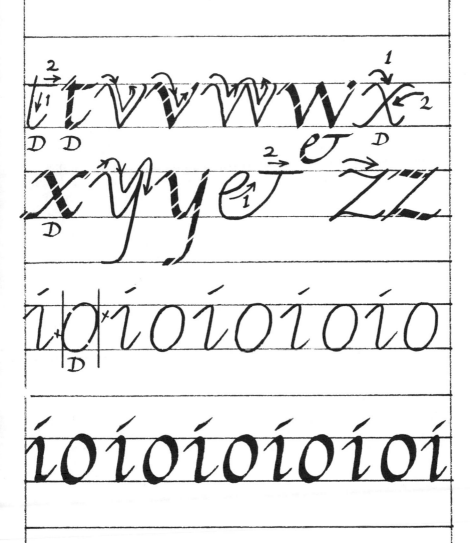

PLATE 4.

Relate *a, d, g, q, b, p, c,* and *e* to *o*. The bases of the bowls of *a, d, g,* and *q* are narrower than the base of *o*. The tops of the bowls of *b* and *p* are narrower than the top of *o*. Both *c* and *e* are a little wider at the base than is *o*. Make all these bowls slope 5° from the vertical. Compare with the *o* on Plate 3, line 3.

Use the same counter (inside paper) for *a, d, g, q, b,* and *p*. See Plate 5, large (B-4) letters. Counters are marked with a figure 1.

Using B-4 guide lines for the top, and B-3 guide lines for the lower 3 lines, write a page of *linoa*.

Note: Do not hurry with this exercise. Be severely critical of your letters. Note (1) pen-angle, (2) slope, (3) width, (4) branching and (5) completely *closed* bowls of *a, d, g,* and *q*—closed *before* the pen is lifted to make the stems. The bowls of *b* and *p* are also closed, even without the overlapping stems. If you lift the pen too soon, the branchings will not be similar and you will have broken the Italic rhythm.

Inspect each letter to see that it is like *o*, the part of the curve farthest left must be low; the part of the curve farthest to the right is high. (Students are often careless with *b* and *p* in this regard.)

Note that the space between words is a little less than the width of *n*. Spacing between letters is difficult. Parallel lines are farther apart than a curve and a straight line. Two curves are closest. Try to get the total space between letters optically even.

If you are not especially careful with *e*, it will fall backwards, sloping to the left rather than to the right. In making the second stroke, the "eye" of *e*, pull to the right at the top, and make a graceful loop, joining the first stroke above the halfway point between writing line and waist line.

4. o as a basic Italic letter.

Q O q adgq OO p bp

lioadgqbpoce
B-4 nib

o aid paid lap gale ail
gape pole bog lope o
dip big paper cage oo
B-3 nib

4

PLATE 5.

In writing the four lines of this exercise, study the spacing between the letters. To repeat, two curves are closest, a curve and a
straight are farther apart, and two straights are farthest apart. The
width of the space between words is slightly less than the width of n.
Note the difficulty of the r, y combination in the last word. To avoid
large holes between r's, keep the ear of r short. Look at book printing
types, either Roman or Italic, and see how very narrow the r's are
made. Then begin the y slightly under the ear of r.

Note that the counters of a and g at the top of Plate 5 are indicated
with a figure 1. The counters of d and q should be like those of a and g.
The inner counter of h should be like those of n and u, indicated here
with a figure 2. Note the exterior triangular counters indicated with a
figure 3. These triangles should be approximately the same size and
shape in a, b, d, g, h, k, m, n, p, q, r, u, and y—in all, thirteen similar
exterior triangular counters.

Notice that when you write, the trail of black ink gives form to
the untouched paper inside the letter and between the letters. A letter
is mostly untouched paper. There is very little ink on a written or
printed page.

There are no letters in an ink bottle because there are no designed
areas of untouched paper. So, make a habit of watching counters, interspaces between letters, and spaces between lines.

Think of your page as being a continuum of letters and untouched
paper. Watch both.

5. Similar counters & branching.

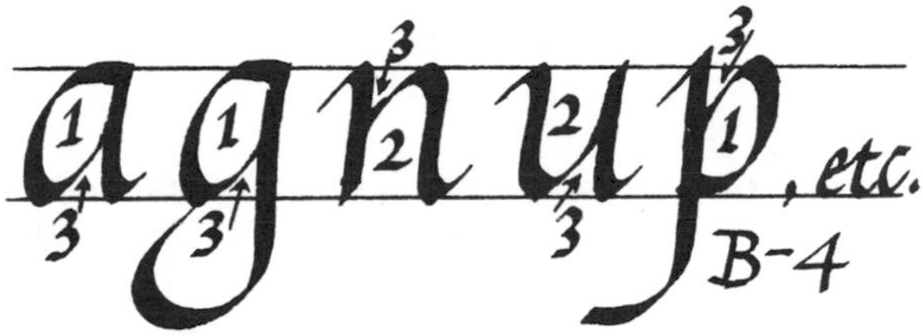

$$a \, g \, n \, u \, p$$, etc.

B-4

Make similar counters as much alike as possible.

adage probe dark

quiz montage one

adjust inmate bid

bark high quarry

B-3

5

PLATE 6.

Note that the crossbars of f and t are just *under* the waist line, but touching it. In these models, the pen-angle is lowered to about 30° from the horizontal to get the crossbars lighter in weight than the verticals.

The curves of f should be full, not angled, and begin and end with horizontal accents. Do not curl the top down or the bottom up, or the rapid movement to the right will be interrupted.

No white paper should show between vertical and crossbar on t. It should never resemble a figure 4. The top of the main stroke of p should extend only one pen-width above the line. *Start the bowl of p at the writing line.* Don't angle s or make it top-heavy. Mid-lines show the slopes of v, w, x, and y. Be very critical of y; don't let it look like ij. And don't make z top-heavy. An alternate t is shown. Keep it *short*.

An alphabet chain alternates n as a link between the letters of the alphabet. For practice, any difficult letter may be used instead of n. Space the letters as they are in the model—as if the chain were one long word.

In the fourth line written with the B-2 nib, the sign following z is called "ampersand." It is based on the letters in *et,* Latin for *and*. Keep it at least as wide as the model. It may be made much wider. Do not overdo the seemingly reverse curve of the horizontal.

An alphabet sentence contains all the letters of the alphabet. This is the shortest one. Write a chain or an alphabet sentence slowly and carefully at least once every day.

Try to make the interspaces between the letters and the spaces between words the same as they are in the model. Try to get them to end as they do in the model, between the vertical margins, which are about $4\frac{1}{4}''$ apart.

Note that the quotation marks are at cap. height, and the semicolon and colon are below center. Question mark and exclamation point are only cap. height. Watch the spacing between letters and between words. Make the lines come out the way they do on the plate.

6. Alphabet chain & AB sentence.

f t p j ff s v w x y z t
B-3↑

B-2↗
nanbncndnenfngnhn

injnknlnmnnnonpnq

nrnsntnunvnwnxny

nze eγ a quick brown

fox jumps over the lazy

dog. "x" ,;: ?! Patience.

Practice critically.
B-2

Keep in mind the 15° pen-angle when you write caps. Otherwise the strongly-built majuscules will disintegrate. Practice will give you straight stems and horizontals and full curves. Be relaxed. Give yourself time. *Absolutely essential* are the width groups. Memorize the widths— *in your hand* as well as in your head.

The first group: O, C, D, G, and Q are about as wide as they are tall. Most of the letters are proportioned (width to height) as they were in the original North Semitic proto-alphabet of about 3500 years ago. The width to height relationships are the result of centuries of intelligent designing; so it would be pointless to tamper with these proportions. Be certain that the horizontals on D are thinner than the vertical stem. If not, your pen-angle is not flat enough.

Lift the upper arm of G and lower the bottom arm. The arm and the straight stroke of the lower right hand part, should form an imaginary line sloping 5° from the vertical.

The 4/5 width of the second group will come with critical practice. The thin crossbar of H rests on a midline between cap. line and writing line. H may be *slightly* narrower in the middle than at top and bottom. The crossbar on A must be low—the width of the bar below the midline. Putting it lower than this makes the letter look "arty"; avoid it. The letter slope should be the same 5° throughout the alphabet; so be careful of V, X, and Y. Determine their slope as you would in writing the lower case counterparts. (See the large letters at the top of Plate 6.) The diagonal of N has a *very slight* reverse curve.

Give Z special care. Study the model carefully. Do not exaggerate the reverse curve of the arms. Keep Z at $7\frac{1}{2}$ pen-widths.

The arms of K meet a little above the midline and the two arms make a 90° angle with each other.

The mid-part of B rests on top of the point halfway between cap. line and writing line. The mid-arm of E rests on top of this midline. The second arm of F rests just *under* this midline. So does the horizontal at the lower part of the bowl of P. The descender on J drops only *halfway down* towards the descender line.

The top horizontals of B, D, P, and R, just before the curve begins, may "shoulder up" slightly.

Do not make R resemble K. Keep the thin mid-horizontal. The diagonal tail of R begins where horizontal meets curve, not to the left.

7. Plain Italic Capitals

I. Wide:
7½ pen widths

Note 15° pen angle

¹Q² O ₂G¹   ¹D²

OCD

II. Width — 4/5 height.

₂G¹₃   ¹Q²₃   ¹L³₃l₃   ¹A³₂   ¹N²₃

GQ·HAN

²T¹   ¹U²   ¹V²   X²   ¹Y²   ¹Y₂

TUVXYY

III·Narrow—Width—half height

Z   ¹K²   ¹B²₃   ¹E²₃   ¹F²₃   J   ¹P²

ZK·BEFJP

B-4

7

S should have full curves, the upper counter being only a *little* smaller than the lower counter. Lift the top arm toward the cap. line; straighten the diagonal spine, and lower the bottom arm toward the writing line, but keep the curves rich and full. Make the letter slope 5° to the right.

The width of *M* is slightly more than its height. *M* is our widest letter; *W*, the same width, is really a monogram made up of two letters, as its name indicates.

The width of *M* is due to its central "V." Be certain that it slopes 5°. The first and third strokes are not parallel; neither are the second and fourth. Think of the first and fourth strokes as sloping but slightly outward from the central "V." In pulling down the fourth stroke, focus your eyes on the point of the "V," and with peripheral vision, pull the stroke down so that the two lower counters are equal. Make the first and third strokes of *M* thinner than the second and fourth strokes. The point of the "V" part of *M* is generally a *little* above the writing line. Let diagonal strokes overlap, whether *V, M, N,* or *W.*

Strokes at head of *A* and also head and foot of *N* should overlap.

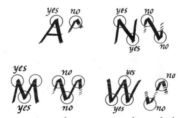

Each of the two majuscule ampersands and the flourished minuscule ampersand which follows can be written with a single stroke, but only after one has practiced the multiple stroke versions. Start at the *x* and continue in the direction of the arrow.

Do not let the *o* of *York* be too close to the *Y.* Keep some air circulating between caps. and the lower case letters which follow.

OHIO is an excellent word to practice. Round *O's* and the straights of *H* and *I* are difficult, but instead of worrying about your difficulty with them, practice them on scratch pads whenever you have a free moment. In time you will have them.

8. Plain Italic Capitals – more'.

IV. Width-height +

LRS·MW

I & & &

OHIO·N

Note steeper pen-angle

York·OH

PLATE 9.

In this exercise see if you can (1) maintain proper widths of caps.; (2) then switch from caps. at a $15°$ pen-angle to lower-case at a $45°$ pen-angle.

Do not let double-counter letters like *B* be top-heavy.

Push with thumb and pull with fingers before writing caps. Then pull with thumb and push with fingers before writing lower-case letters. (It is less trouble than pushing the cap. button and the release on a typewriter.) Keep the caps. at $7\frac{1}{2}$ pen widths in height.

Do not crowd the lower-case letter close to the capital. Caps. are architectural; they need space around them.

Keep the caps. as plain as possible. Any attempts at "fancy" strokes will make the caps. fall apart.

Do not let *Z* be taller than the other capitals, and keep it plain but not rigid.

Aix Beersheba Colophon
Dublin Ely Florence Ghent
Gubbio Hebron Innisfree
Jerusalem Kyoto La Mesa
Oxford Naples Perugia
Qemoy Rome Spoleto
Treviso Ulm Vicenza
Xanadu York Winchester
Yuma & Zion

B

9

PLATE 10.

Keep the width groups. The slab serifs or swashes (flourishes) do not affect the basic letter width. Keep slabs flat (and thin) and keep the flourishes strong and full. Don't let them fall limply over the verticals. Try to get optically even spaces within the word *PORTLAND*. It should not break into *PORTL* and *AND*. Watch pen-angles and spacing.

The arm serif, or finishing stroke at the end of the upper arm of *C* is made by twisting the pen on its upper right corner. See *G* and *S*.

Keep the arms of *C* straightened toward their guidelines. The top must not dip, the lower arm must not curl up steeply. The slab serifs are *slightly* concave; "cupped" is the printer's term.

The lower right-hand corner of *N* is pointed. Go up on the left corner of the nib when finishing the diagonal. When finishing the right vertical, go up on the right corner. See *V, M, N,* and *W* below. If ink does not flow into white spaces, shove it with corner of pen.

MNVW

Note the right head-serif on *M,* above. After coming down on the third stroke, lengthen the left side of the top with a hairline and then with a flat pen move to the right and curve left and down. This is a simple way to make the complex looking head serif for the fourth stroke.

Notice that *V, W, X,* and *Y* are more handsome if the serifs do not extend much into the counter areas. Think of the serifs as half-serifs, barely entering the counters. The terminal foot serifs of *A* and *M* may be half-serifs. Do not let the foot serif of the first stroke of *A* crowd conspicuously into the counter. The same holds for *K* and *R*.

The serif on the upper diagonal of *K* requires a quick change in pen-angle. A second stroke over it completes the serif.

serif on upper diagonal of K

Keep the horizontal part of the flourished head serifs on *H, K, L, M, N, U,* and *V very* straight and horizontal. (See the lower half of Plate 10.)

10. *Capitals: Slab-serif & Swash*

CDG·HATN

UVXYZK·B

EFJLPRS·M"

MW·& &

Swash cap. variants: ANUV

XYYKLM

WHRVYZ

PORTLAND

B-2

PLATE 11.

Keep the capitals strong and graceful. Changing pen sizes from one exercise to another (or within a single exercise) is difficult, but it will accelerate your progress. "Size is absolute," said Edward Johnston. Letters are not just enlarged or reduced automatically and in exact proportion. Small letters are a little rounder, wider, and heavier in proportion, than large letters. Train your eye to see this.

The shaded line above the first T is there to remind you that T should be only $7\frac{1}{2}$ pen widths in height. It can be less and be handsome. *But do not exceed the recommended height of $7\frac{1}{2}$ pen widths.*

The light touch necessary in good writing seldom appears in printed reproductions of pen work. One has to see the original writing. The printing process thickens the hairlines.

Try to achieve a flower-light touch in writing this word list. Before writing this exercise, review what is written about touch in the comments on Plates 1, 2, and 3. See that the branching occurs at mid-point and that the external triangular counters are alike. Be especially careful of the curves in *b, p,* and *e;* relate them properly to a perfect *o.*

Write at even a slower rate of speed when you begin with the Broad and Medium nibs. Only after long practice can you accelerate with any safety.

11. Slab Serif Italic Caps. Word List.

The This That Those These
Aster Bellflower Calypso
Daffodill Edelweiss Forsythia
Goldenrod Heather Iris Jasmin
Kniphofia Lily Marigold
Narcissus Orchid Peach Quince
Rue Snowdrop Tulip Urbinia
Violet Windflower Xeran-
themum Yarrow Zinnia
Anemone Windflower
Yellow=bells

11   B

PLATE 12.

The Arabic-Indian figures came into Europe in the 12th century —brought by the Moors in Spain. Their origin explains why the figures are difficult to harmonize with our alphabet—which is North Semitic, Greek and Latin.

Beginners tend to make the figures too narorw—especially the *4*. Never crowd them. Like majuscules they need wide spacing; but like minuscules they have extruders (ascenders and descenders). But keep the extruders short. The zero is wider than Italic *o*.

The *2* is wider than you think. Note the alignment of terminals at the left in *2, 3, 5,* and *9,* which determine the 5° slope of the figures —also the alignment on the right side of *6*. The downstroke of *7* should not come as far left as the beginning of the top. Keep the figures from being tall. If they are short, wide, and widely spaced, they will be handsome.

Note the extreme shortness of the "small caps." (5½ pen widths) in the writing with a Medium nib—the *B. C., A. D.,* and *P. M.*

Especially when writing to someone in continental Europe, distinguish between figures 1 and 7 by putting a foot serif on 1 and a tick on 7. A European is likely to read our 7 as a 1.

12. Italic Old Style Figures

1206834579

B-3

1206834579

Note: figures are widely spaced.

1206834579 Broad

7423 S.E. 31 Avenue
Portland, Oregon
97202

July 4, 1776.   1500 B.C.

A.D. 1066.   7:30 P.M.

5½. $4.25.   15¢.   1st

Medium

12

PLATES 13 AND 14.

Teachers should present only the best. Students have enough difficulty without having to make choices, especially when their experience has not yet given them a basis for value judgments.

These joins are quite fool-proof. They are the only *safe* ones. Horizontal joins, unless out of *f* and *t* and into a letter having an entrance, like *n*, tend to disintegrate the alphabet, especially when one is writing rapidly. Joins into ascenders tend to club them or provide distracting loops. Joins into *v, w, x,* and *y* (unless out of *f* or *t*) tend to make unrecognizable counters.

Learn the safe joins now. At your own discretion and depending upon the degree of cursiveness or formality desired, you may introduce the unsafe joins. But wait until after you finish this course.

Give special attention to the pen-angle. It should be up *between 45° and 50°* to the writing line if you are to get a hairline join that is as steep and as thin as it should be. A flatter pen angle will push the letters too far apart or will make the diagonal join too prominent, too heavy. Remember what is said above about touch: almost lift the pen off the paper in getting this light diagonal join.

Try using the hairline diagonal join to establish the norm for the space between letters.

In Plate 14 an unbroken line indicates that all letters above it are joined. The vertical indicates the pen lift required in writing a two stroke letter. Thus the word *at* is joined, but two strokes are required. Count the horizontals and verticals to check the number of strokes required in writing the word.

This underlining is useful in classroom drills, in which the teacher gives the word and writes it on the blackboard at the same time that the students write it. The students can check the number of pen strokes at a glance and see immediately if they have used the recommended safe joins.

The medium guide line sheet is here recommended for use with the Broad nib, because it is customary in rapid personal writing to use a scale of four pen widths instead of the more formal scale of five pen widths.

13. The Safe Joins

→← nen eimntu (join either way)
→ acdfhl (to the right only)
← jngoprs (to the left only)
—○ bgkqvwxyz (no safe joins)

nan bn cn dnen fn gn hn in jn
nkn ln mn nn on pn qn rn sn tn
nun vn wn xn yn z.
a quick brown fox jumps over the
lazy dog. (Joins: ui, fo, ump,
er, he.) moment minimum
monomania communion also
comm an dment mono tony

Medium

13

one[3] at[2] ate[3] nun[1] mum[1] monomania[5]

minimum[2] moment[4] communion[3]

nomination[6] minute[4] lazy[4] gnome[4]

mountains[4] peak[6] cliff[5] fault[5] butte[5]

scarp[5] fireweed[4][6] bear[4] grass[4] riprap[6]

chimney[3] scree[5] mattock[5] shovel[6] axe[5]

jack[4] hammer[3] powder[7] pack[5] trail[4]

diamond[6] hitch[4] lodgepole[10] pine[4]

Sitka[5] spruce[7] red fir[2] hemlock[5] fire[4]

vine[3] maple[5] Oregon[7] lily[3] trillium[5]

Clackamas[7] lily[3] Iris[3] tenax[6] dew[3]

Broad – 4 p.w.
(Medium guide)

14

PLATE 15.

This arcade exercise is difficult, but of great importance. Block off all finger action and use *only your wrist* in writing the narrow elliptical arches of the arcade. See if you are mistakenly flexing your fingers.

The exits of *h, m,* and *n* should be ignored at present. Get the arches and *let* the exits be spiky. The tops of letters are read, anyhow. If you anticipate the exits, finger action will begin too soon and angle the last stroke of *m,* and the shoulders of both *h,* and *n.*

Practice the arcade rapidly at first, to give your fingers no chance to interfere. When you can write the elliptical shoulders of *h, m,* and *n* with wrist action only, then try combining wrist and finger action in the exits.

The moment you find that you are getting the arcade with wrist action, try using it in a word—such as *moment.* Whenever an *h, m,* or *n* goes spiky, go back to the arcade. Do not do any exercise in a thoughtless, mechanical manner. Keep alert every moment to what is happening and mend the mistakes without repeating them.

Few students acquire the arcade at once. Take as much time as you require, and do not become impatient. If it takes a month to get it, then be happy that it takes only a month.

For this exercise, use a Medium nib with the Fine guide lines.

15. Arcade

mmm mmm mmm mm mmm mmm mm mm mm mm

mmm mm mm mm mm mm mm mm mmm

mm m m m m m m m m m m m

nn mn mn mmn mn m mn nn

mum mum mum nun nun nun

moment communion command

commandment monomania

mountain anonymous minute

minimum hammer nomination

memorandum monotone murmur

amusement ominous immune

imminent mime gnome manual

grammarian ornament gnomon

imitation homonym hymn none

nonsense anonymity magnanimity

Medium – at 4 pen widths

15   (Fine guide lines)

PLATE 16.

These alternate letter forms are for more graceful rhythms in semi-formal work, such as awards, announcements, and greetings.

Note the *curve* of the vertical into a slim horizontal foot serif in *F, K, M,* and *R*. The same curve joins the vertical of *L* into the arm. Don't make an abrupt angle, if you want the smoothest movement.

The *Y* is difficult, because the first stroke makes a quick, seemingly awkward, break a little above the writing line. The right-hand stroke slides into the first stroke so that it is impossible to tell which diagonal produced the descending part of the letter.

The diagonal of Q starts on top of the writing line.

Make certain that caps. with double counters are not top-heavy; make the upper counter *only a little* smaller. (Note B, E, H, K, R, S, X.) Keep the lower counters of *M* equal. Keep the thin stems of *N* parallel. Try to keep the letter-slope at a uniform 5°.

Do not let the tail of Q collide with any letter that follows it.

Keep the slightly diagonal flourishes to *p* and *q* as straight as possible—until the *end,* when you can flick the pen up or down quickly.

The angled descender of *g* should be rounded at the turn, and note the flattened bowl and its slightly sloping axis:

The push heads of *b, d, h, k,* and *l* should be *curved.* Do not permit an angle in the lower side of the curve at the top.

The flourished finishing strokes on the ends of the *p* and *q* descenders must *not* slope away from the line, i.e., *not* from upper left to lower right. The diagonal of the lower case *q* (the one like a small version of the capital) should be straight until the very end, which, turning upward in a slight (and graceful) curve, leads the eye back to the writing line. The round lower case *g* should slope, and the lower bowl should be quite *flattened,* with an axis tilting from lower left to upper right.

16. Alternate Finishing Strokes

F K L M R Y Y Q

b d h k l p q n u g n y g

B-2

Aster Edelweiss For=

sythia Kinnikinnic

Lily Marigold Narcissus

Ranunculus Quamoclit

Yarrow Zinnia·Crocus

Indian Paint Brush

B

PLATE 17.

The free rhythm and flourishes of the top five lines are dangerous. The movement is too active, too busy, to make a readable text. Use it only for titles or "display lines" on bulletins and notices. One phrase or one line of this in a larger size, is probably quite enough.

The lower seven lines are to receive most study at this stage of your learning. The style is eminently readable and rhythmical. Make it the model for your rapid hand and use it even for subordinate lines on posters, notices, etc.

To develop a sense of rhythm and to develop skill in actual (not just "visual") movement, work on these contrasts: move slower on the heavy stems, quicker on the up-swing hairlines. Use little pressure on thick strokes, less pressure as the lines get thinner, and almost leave the paper on the swift up-stroke hairlines. Contrasts of pressure, friction, speed, and visual thickness can combine to produce rich rhythmical contrasts and variations in beat. At first exaggerate these contrasts. Study the demonstrations.

Working to music (such as Mozart's *Symphony No. 40 in G Minor*) and concentrating on *listening* will teach you much about possibilities of rhythm in pen touch and movement. And by listening rather than watching the pen fearfully, you may find that the tactile and kinetic images of the letters are safely in your hand—and you can stop worrying. Writing with the eyes closed is also a good test of what your hand and wrist know and whether you can trust them.

A master writer is aware of what his hand is doing, but he can think of the meaning of the text instead of shepherding his fingers.

17. Rhythm

calligraphy paleography
eagle flight gillyflower
glyptic photography style
quality quiz alphabetic
legato rhythm free flowing
B

mythology symbolism calligraphy
paleography alphabet syllabary
paragraph punctuation quotation
bibliography bibliophile typophile
majuscule minuscule versal initial
old style figures layout design letters
literature literacy form information
Medium - 4 p.w.
(Fine guide lines)

PLATE 18.

Roman Capitals make up our most difficult alphabet. But as Gian-francesco Cresci wrote in 1570, it is "the queen of all the alphabets," and "he who can write Roman Capitals can write anything." I have found that with advanced students, they do not want to write any other alphabet. And Edward Johnston wrote, "When in doubt, use Roman Capitals."

Roman Capitals only were used with the Italic minuscules in Italy during the Renaissance. So in that sense, they are necessary in a course in Italic. Swashes were used by Arrighi in 1522, but the letters remained vertical—and kept to their width groups.

Only critical practice over a period of time will give you the Roman Capitals. Take it easy, and do not grow impatient. In time with many periods of critical practice, the verticals will be true and straight, the arms will be horizontal and not flabby, and the curves will be full. Just *practice critically*.

The serifs must not be too heavy—a most common error in beginners' work. Keep them *slightly* concave.

The terminal serif at the top arms of *C, G, E, F,* and *S* is made by a rapid twist of the pen on its upper corner, combined with a downward pull at a very steep pen-angle. Practice will do it.

Get a slight shouldering to *B, D, P,* and *R*.

The left foot serif on *A* is written as follows:

Using the left corner of the nib, pull the first stroke (the fillet) to the left (1); place the pen's edge flat on the paper and make the slightly cupped stroke (2) to the right; then go up on the right corner and draw the curved fillet (3) up into the diagonal.

The right foot serif begins with the curve at (4). Lift the pen, place the left corner up on the diagonal, draw the fillet (5) and continue with the cupped stroke—overlapping (4).

The foot serifs of *M* and *N* are produced similarly.
The right head serif of *N* is made by first pulling the cupped
stroke to the right (6); lift the pen and draw the fillet with the left
corner (7) and lift again, then with the right corner draw the right
fillet (8). Now proceed with the thin down-stroke.

In small pen sizes (Medium or Fine), full head, foot and arm serifs
are *suggested mostly* by pressing and twisting the pen lightly into the
paper.

The following alphabet sentence was written with a Medium nib.
The letters are less than an eighth of an inch in height—about the size
of 10 point printing types. Obviously they require a feather touch.

QUICK BROWN FOX JUMPS
OVER THE LAZY DOG

O C D G Q

İHANTU

VXYZKB

EFJLPRSI

MW &

B-4

PLATE 19.

Do not let the diagrams of plates 19-21 intimidate you, even if your knowledge of geometry is somewhat stale or non-existent. The rectangles, margins, and the use of the diagonal for enlarging or reducing, are all much easier than making letters. Go through the steps slowly and take it easy. Do it repeatedly until you find it easy and satisfying.

The formula $\dfrac{A+B-D}{6} = 2$ units was developed by one of my gifted students who was a chemistry major. I call it the "Joseph Feinblatt formula" in his honor, for it is quite ingenious.

To avoid awkward fractions, use an engineer's rule (on which inches are divided into tenths), a centimeter rule, which is available in most stationery stores, or a printer's pica rule.

The golden rectangle and quarto rectangle are proportions, and not particular sizes. Quarto pages are common in books of poetry and are especially good for sonnets.

The rectangle (A B C D) at the bottom of the page is a horizontal golden rectangle. Draw it in the lower left-hand corner of a large sheet of paper. Extend the base to the right and the left side vertically. Draw the diagonal as shown and extend it as far as your paper will allow. A horizontal and vertical through any particular point on that diagonal, as at X or Y, will give a golden rectangle.

If one wants a horizontal golden rectangle with a height of say 17", then mark 17" off on the extension of AB. If AW is 17", then WY is the width of the new golden rectangle.

19. Single-sheet Layout

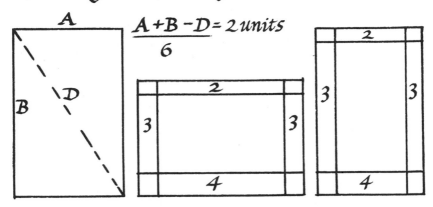

$$\frac{A + B - D}{6} = 2 \text{ units}$$

Text area about 52% of total area.

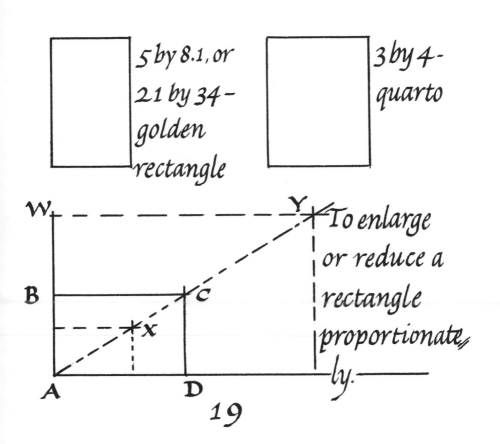

5 by 8.1, or 21 by 34 – golden rectangle

3 by 4 – quarto

To enlarge or reduce a rectangle proportionately. ——

19

PLATE 20.

Root two and root three rectangles are developed out of a square, as shown in the diagrams at the top of Plate 20. EFCD is a root two rectangle, and GHCD is a root three rectangle. These various rectangles have been very popular with graphic designers for many centuries.

The "canon" is the recent rediscovery of Jan Tschichold of Basle, Switzerland. It was universally used in European shop practice throughout the late Middle Ages and early Renaissance. See Tschichold's essay "Non-Arbitrary Proportions of Page and Type Area" in *Calligraphy and Palaeography,* Faber and Faber, 1965.

The canon proves (if necessary) that William Morris was right when he insisted on the historical practice of designing a book using the two pages of an opening as the unit rather than the single page. The canon may be worked only on the two pages of a book opening.

The diagram at the bottom of Plate 20 shows the opening of a book made up of golden rectangles.

Start by drawing the diagonals AC and BD. Then draw ED and EC. At the crossing, F, erect a perpendicular. It cuts the head of the page at G. Then draw a line from G to the crossing at H. That diagonal cuts EC at I. A horizontal through I gives us the head margin. Drop a perpendicular from J. That gives the fore edge margin. This vertical cuts the diagonal EC at K, and a horizontal through K gives the foot margin. Drop a perpendicular from I. That is the inner, or gutter, margin. Copy this on the "verso" page, the page to the left. (The page on the right is a "recto" page.)

20. Book Design

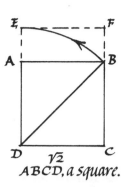

ABCD, a square.
EFCD, a Root
Two rectangle.

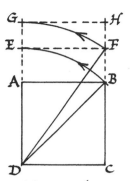

A Root Three
(√3) rectangle.

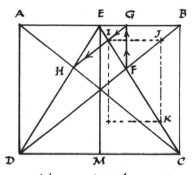

Golden rectangles as pages,
5:8.1, or 21:34, ratio

The Canon: Draw diagonals as shown. Erect a perpendicular at F. Draw a
line from G to H. It crosses
E-C at I, which establishes
top & inner margins. A
horizontal from I establishes
the outer side margin; & a
line dropped from J, the bottom margin

PLATE 21.

To make any of the traditional rectangles (including the popular 2:3) and then to try to fit your writing to the page size, can be a disheartening and time-wasting task. Good craftsmen may be, as Johnston says, good guessers, but guessing involves hit-or-miss, trial-and-error procedures, which are poor shop practice.

At least *know* what the efficient time- and labor-saving shop practices are. Like scale, they give you a norm, which can, at least, be a point of departure.

By using Plate 21 you can write out in your own inimitable style and spacing, the longest line in any poem you want to put into booklet form. The length of that line can give you the page sizes—and after drawing the canon, you have the classic margins.

The canon has been worked on ABCD, giving the margins. The diagonal DB has been extended as far as it will go.

You can project *any* measurement taken on the opening if you mark it off on the BC vertical, and project a line through it from D. Thus HG is the line length on ABCD; if you mark off this length on BC, it will be CK. CL is the same as MB, the *page* width. A diagonal from D is extended through L.

Now, if your line length is DJ, extend it horizontally until it cuts the extension of DK. PQ is *your* line length; then PN is the new page *width* and PO the new page *height*. Draw the opening on scrap paper, work the canon, and you are ready to make the book.

Some students panic at all this, but with concentration, patience, and careful step-by-step procedure, even the slowest students finally get it. Keep redrawing the diagram until you see how it works. You *can* see that on the resulting book opening all details are in the same proportion, one to another, that they are in the original small diagram. Your personal line length has only produced all other dimensions in the proper proportion.

Do not worry if the paper is so thin that a "shadow" appears from the writing on the other side. Many parchments are this thin. Just see that all lines are equally distant from the head of the page, and that you *always* write on a third line down. Lines must always "back up" perfectly, so that no shadow of body height letters appears in the wrong interlinear spaces.

All titles should be the same distance from the top. Usually, one

To lay out a book of poems with a page proportion of 2:3. In the lower left-hand corner of a piece of poster board ca. 22"x17", draw the book opening. By means of the Canon, draw the page margins. Mark off the width of the text (or line length), EF, at C-K. Mark off the width of page (M-B) at C-L. Extend lines from D through B.L.K, etc.

❦ Now, the poems. Write out the longest line. Let's say that its length is D-J. Draw a horizontal through J until it in= tersects the extension of D-K at Q. To take your line= length, the page will have a width P=N and height O-P. Using the Canon, find the margins—OR. to save time, mark the margins on B-C and extend lines to O-P. ❦ Such charts can be made for each page ratio.

L (C-L is the width of the page — M-B)

K (C-K is the line length — E-F)

Book opening with single page

Book Design - 2
21

skips a *line* (called a "white" line) between the title and the first line of the poem.

Colored "Art Papers" make good cover stock for booklets. Refer to books in the book list for more information. The bibliography is only a beginning, but it is a good one, and it will take you a long way.

The question of what paper to use in book making is a lengthy one and we cannot take it up in this introductory booklet.

You can order 17" x 22" sheets of Strathmore "Parchment" (*not* a skin and thankfully *not* "vegetable parchment") through your local art supply stores or paper companies.

See Plates 22 and 23 for examples of work done by using these traditional shop practices.

The exhibition notice is reduced from a width of $21\frac{3}{8}''$. It is a horizontal golden rectangle. The margins were found by the Feinblatt formula (see comment on Plate 19).

Notice that all four margins (indicated by broken lines) are touched. The first line touches top and left side margin. The bottom line touches right side and bottom margin.

The area bounded by the four margins is approximately the classic fifty per cent of the total area. With enough experience, one can guess at margin and text area proportions.

The pens used were Speedball C-O, C-1, and fountain pen B-4.

The notice was written twice to save time and effort. The lines of the first writing were cut apart. Then each line was placed in position just above the proper ruled guide lines, and the final writing freely copied on the ruled lines. The cut out line may be held in place by the left hand or by architect's draughting tape. (See the reproduction.)

Another method is to get the first writing correct—by pasting up, if necessary—and then to use a light-table (heavy glass with light behind it). But with heavy paper or poster board, the first method must be used.

Spelling mistakes or lines that run beyond one's expectations are a waste of effort and of time and materials. The methods suggested here will enable the writer to remain relaxed while working efficiently and accurately.

The single page of the booklet measures $8'' \times 10\frac{3}{4}''$. It is a quarto in proportion of width to depth, i.e., $3:4$.

The second line of the poem is the longest and was used on a quarto-extension chart (see Plate 21) to find the page width and height. It was written with a medium nib, using the corresponding guide lines, so that the body height is five pen widths, and the writing lines are fifteen pen widths apart. On the left side of the opening, the bottom line is a little above the bottom margin.

Notice that in book design, all pages begin the same distance from the top edge; and all lines (including the "white" lines, or ones not written on) are fifteen pen widths apart.

Consequently, any line is lined up with a written line or a white line on the opposite page. Also, if a page is held up to light, it will be seen that lines are in the same position on both sides of leaf. This alignment of the front (recto) and back (verso) of leaf is called "backing up."

The Arrighi Club sponsors an

Italic Handwriting

EXHIBITION

April 15–30 The School Library

April 15–30 The School Library

PLATE 22.

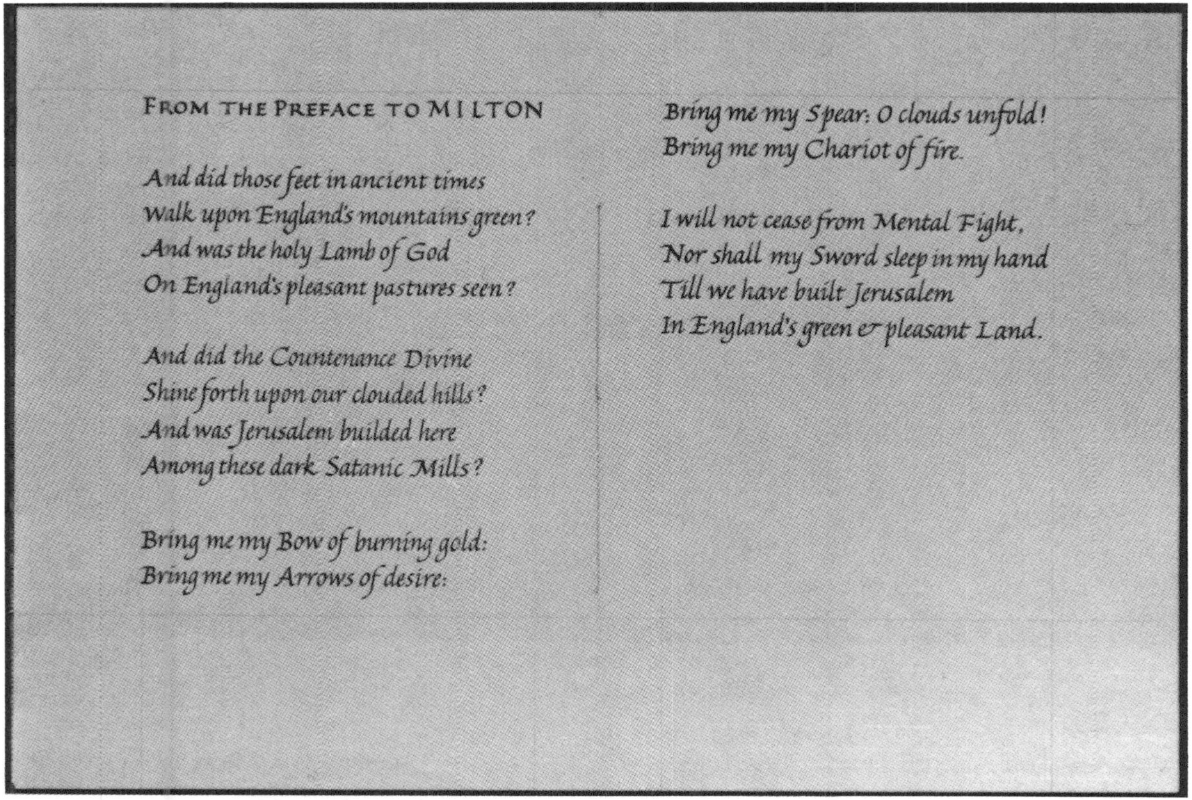

FROM THE PREFACE TO MILTON

And did those feet in ancient times
Walk upon England's mountains green?
And was the holy Lamb of God
On England's pleasant pastures seen?

And did the Countenance Divine
Shine forth upon our clouded hills?
And was Jerusalem builded here
Among these dark Satanic Mills?

Bring me my Bow of burning gold:
Bring me my Arrows of desire:

Bring me my Spear: O clouds unfold!
Bring me my Chariot of fire.

I will not cease from Mental Fight,
Nor shall my Sword sleep in my hand
Till we have built Jerusalem
In England's green & pleasant Land.

PLATE 23.

Fine

Medium

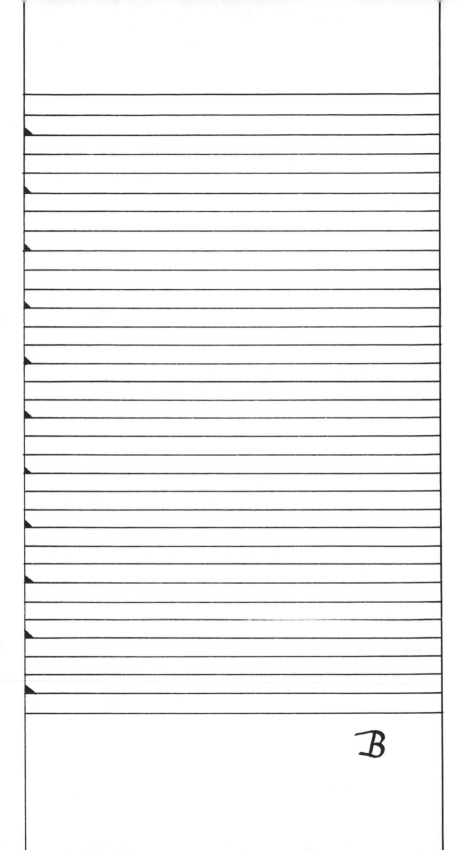

B

B-2

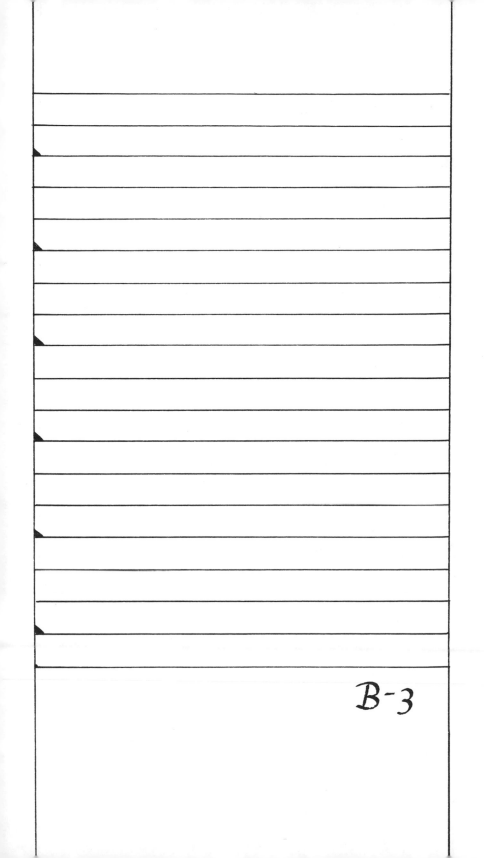

B-3

letter-slope

pen-angle

B-4

TOOLS AND MATERIALS

Platignum Pen Set. "Straight" Italic nibs for right-handed writers and for the left-handed writers who turn the paper 90° clockwise.

Ordinary black fountain pen ink—a dye, not a carbon ink. Pad of $8\frac{1}{2}$″ x 11″ bond paper, unlined.

T-square.

60°-30° 16″ triangle.

7H or 9H pencil.

Drawing board or square of plywood to set in the lap, resting the board against the table. The left edge should be perfectly straight. The T-square slides along this edge. Draw all horizontal lines with the T-square and draw all vertical lines using the triangle, the base resting on the T-square. Then lines will be parallel or perfectly horizontal and vertical.

See Johnston for drawings of a table-top writing desk. A sloping desk is preferable for formal and semi-formal writing. Keep the paper vertical. But in rapid handwriting, write on a horizontal surface; and cant the paper.

RECOMMENDED SUPPLEMENTARY READING

Alfred Fairbank: *A Handwriting Manual.* Faber and Faber, 24 Russell Square, London. Cloth or paper. The text on the modern Italic handwriting movement.

.....................: *A Book of Scripts.* Penguin.
        The Story of Handwriting. Watson-Guptill.

John Howard Benson:. *The First Writing Book, Arrighi's Manual.* Yale University Press. New Haven, Conn. Cloth or paper. The "Chancery Cursive" style of Italic in the Italian high Renaissance. A facsimile and a translation written out in Italic.

Edward Johnston: *Writing and Illuminating and Lettering.* Pitman. The "bible" of the lettering-arts revival.

Dr. A. S. Osley (Editor): *Calligraphy and Palaeography.* Faber and Faber. Essays in honor of Mr. Fairbank. See Jan Tschichold's essay "Non-arbitrary Proportions of Page and Type Area." Many other essays of importance to writers of Italic.

Donald M. Anderson: *The Art of Written Forms: The Theory and Practice of Calligraphy.* Holt, Rinehart and Winston, Inc. 383 Madison Ave., New York, N. Y. 10017.

Fairbank and Wolpe: *Renaissance Handwriting.* Faber and Faber, London.

James Wardrop: *The Script of Humanism.* Oxford.

Crump and Jacob: *The Legacy of the Middle Ages.* E. A. Lowe, "Handwriting." Oxford at the Clarendon Press. The lower case alphabet and Italic as contributions of the Middle Ages.

Berthold L. Ullman: *Ancient Writing and Its Influence.* Cooper Square Publishers, Inc. New York.

E. M. Catich: *The Trajan Inscription in Rome.* The Catfish Press, St. Ambrose College, Davenport, Iowa.

.................: *The Origin of the Roman Serif.* The Catfish Press, St. Ambrose College, Davenport, Iowa.

Maury Nemoy: *The Study of Letterforms: Typographic.* The Scorpio Press, 11558 Kling St., North Hollywood, Calif.

The Journal of the Society for Italic Handwriting.
    Western American Branch of the S. I. H.
        Secretary: Jo Anne Di Sciullo
            6800 S. E. 32nd Ave.
            Portland, Oregon 97202
    Membership and subscription to the quarterly *Journal*, $10.00 per year. Articles on paleography, handwriting, teaching, history — all aspects of Italic script. An invaluable source of information.

John Corderoy: *Bookbinding for Beginners.* Watson-Guptill Publications.

Pauline Johnson: *Creative Bookbinding.* University of Washington Press, Seattle, Washington.

BOOKS OF REPRODUCTIONS

Calligraphy: The Golden Age and Its Modern Revival. Portland Art Museum, Portland, Oregon.

Calligraphy Today. (Edited by Heather Child.) Studio Books, London.

2,000 Years of Calligraphy. Walters Art Gallery, Baltimore, Maryland.